EARTH DAY

COLORING BOOK

LesrubaBooks.com

Published by Lesruba Books

Earth Day is on April 22.

It's a day to think about
how we can help our planet.

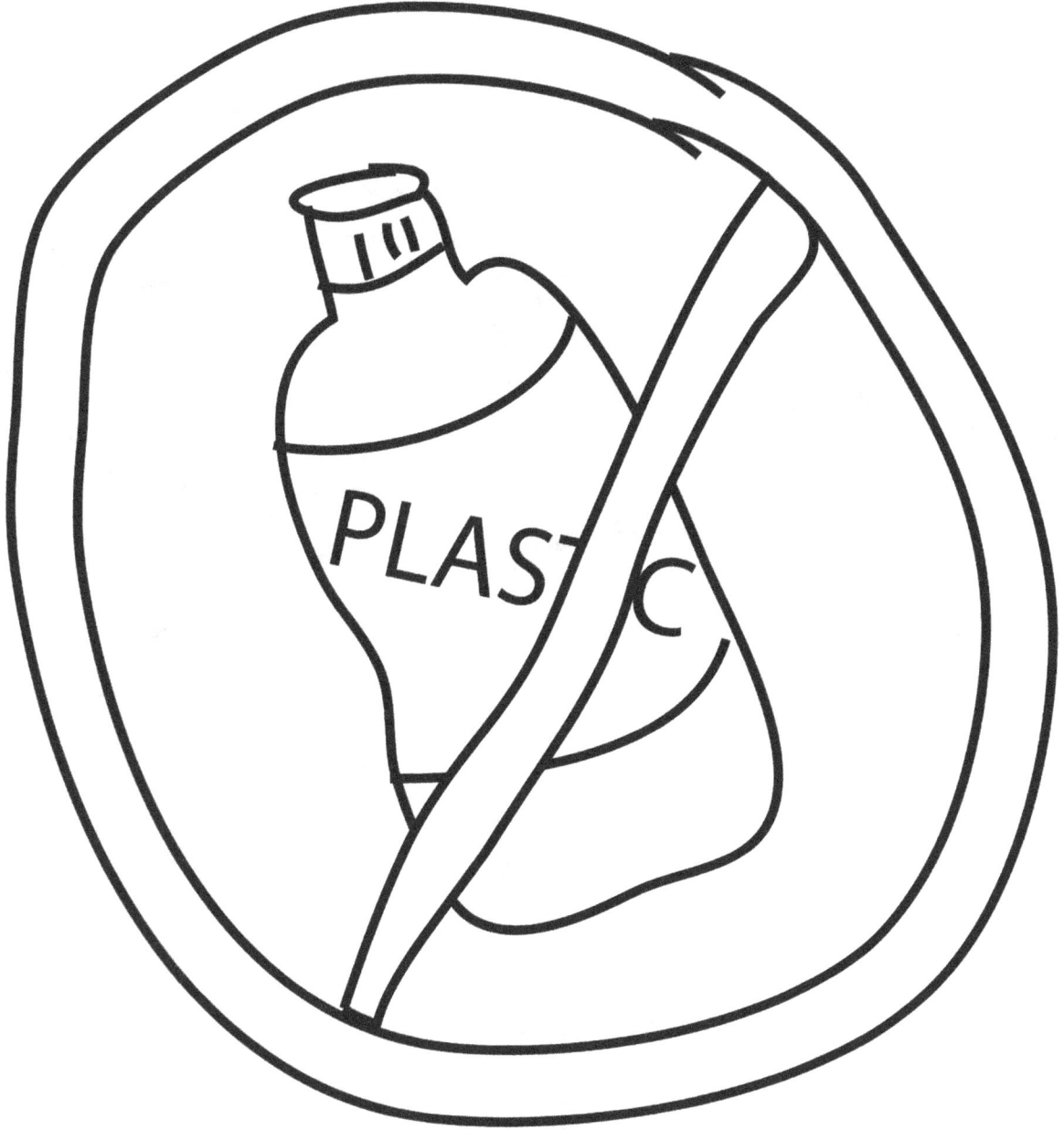

Small changes have a big impact.

Plant a tree.

Turn lights off when you leave a room.

Give a hoot and don't pollute.

Recycle.

Eat fewer animal products.

Bicycle or walk.
Leave the car at home.

Keep our oceans clean.

Use the energy from the sun.

Plant a garden.

Respect Nature.

Eat local foods and produce.

Shut off the water
when brushing your teeth.

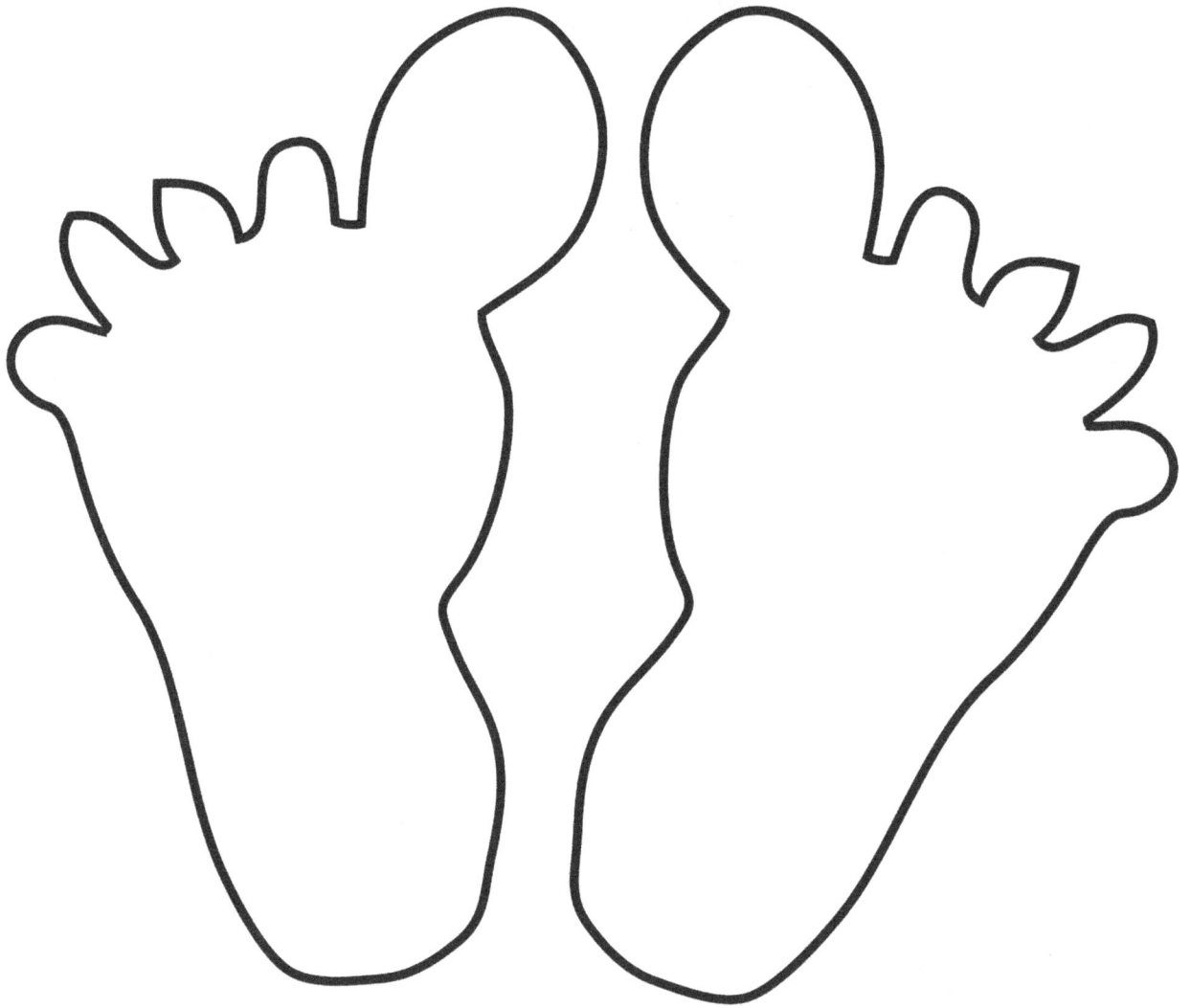

Reduce your carbon footprint.

Go green - It's easy being green.

Green looks good on everyone.

Love the earth every day.

HAPPY

EARTH DAY!

More books by Leslie Nazarian:

A Happy Halloween

Winnie McGoo's Museum Adventure

Woofer Works Out

W is for Woofer

Orelda and Corelda's Ocean Voyage

Orelda and Corelda on Wall Street

Visit us online at
LesrubaBooks.com
and
LesrubaDesigns.com

www.ingramcontent.com/pod-product-compliance
Lightning Source LLC
Chambersburg PA
CBHW080537030426
42337CB00023B/4779